LeTTeRS FRoM MiNTy

AN ~~Imaginative look at the~~ Life AND THougHTs oF A YouNg HaRRieT TuBMaN

Written and illustrated by fourth and fifth grade students of Gateway Christian Academy, Fort Lauderdale, Florida.

ORIGINAL COVER
Scholastic Inc.   New York Toronto London Auckland Sydney New Delhi Hong Kong

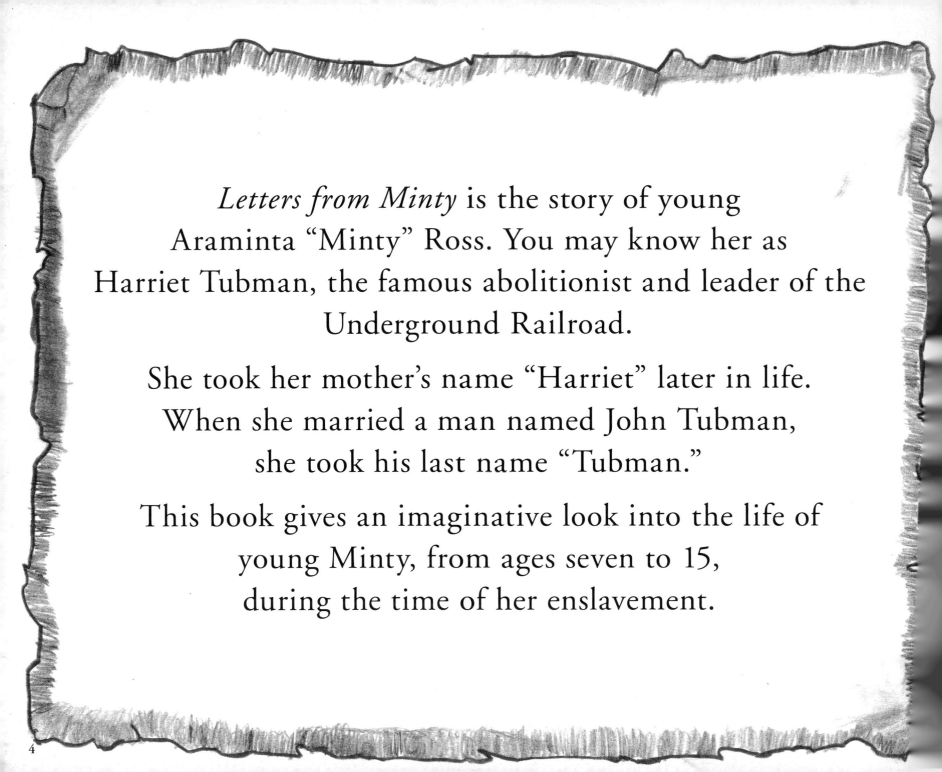

Letters from Minty is the story of young Araminta "Minty" Ross. You may know her as Harriet Tubman, the famous abolitionist and leader of the Underground Railroad.

She took her mother's name "Harriet" later in life. When she married a man named John Tubman, she took his last name "Tubman."

This book gives an imaginative look into the life of young Minty, from ages seven to 15, during the time of her enslavement.

We dedicate this book to the
faculty and staff of
Gateway Christian Academy,
who helped us to dream big and gave
wings to our dreams.

January, 1827

Dear Friend,

My name is Araminta, but my folks call me Minty. I was born on a slave plantation in the state of Maryland. I am a slave, which means I am owned by my master, Edward Brodas. He owns all the slaves on this plantation. Slaves are not allowed to learn to read and write but I did. I hear footsteps coming, I have to go.

Minty

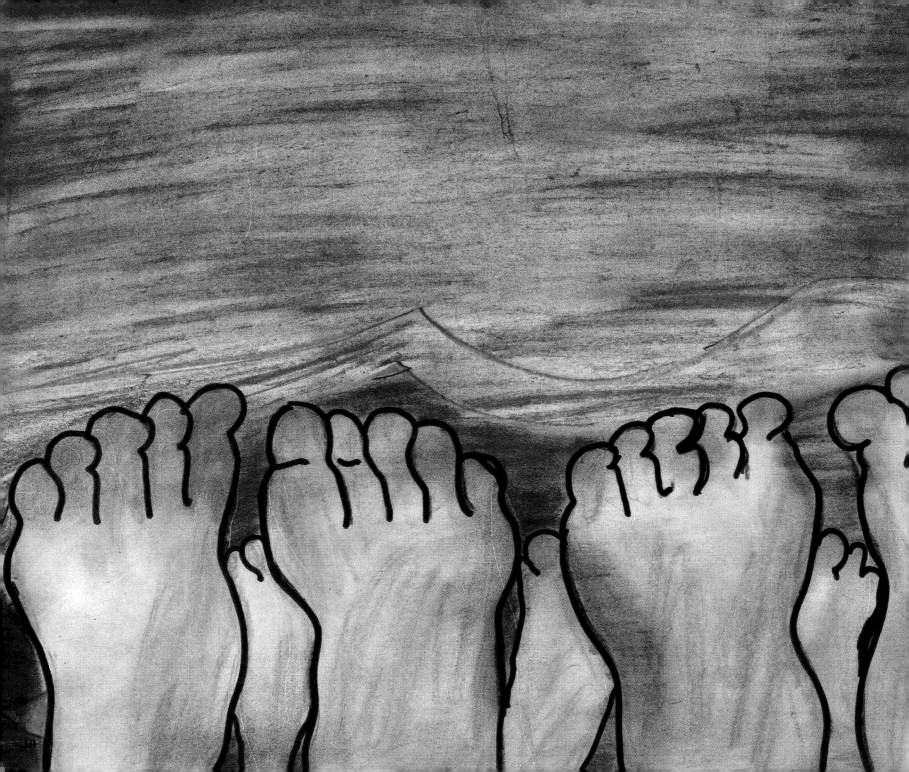

FEBRUARY, 1827

DEAR FRIEND,

DID I TELL YOU I AM SEVEN YEARS OLD? HOW OLD ARE YOU?
IT IS DARK AND DAMP IN THE CABIN WHERE WE SLEEP BUT I
ALWAYS TRY TO GET CLOSE TO OLD RIT AND MY BROTHERS
TO KEEP WARM. WE GIGGLE AND PLAY FOOTSIES UNTIL WE FALL
ASLEEP. I STAY AWAKE MOST TIMES AND DREAM OF NORTH. THEY
SAY IF YOU LIVE THERE, YOU WILL BE FREE, FREE LIKE A BIRD IN
A TREE.

MINTY

March, 1827

Dear Friend,

Master Osborne, the overseer is feeling ill. He had to leave us alone in the cornfields. Old Rit told me to go get a drink of water and rest a few minutes before the overseer returns. I think I will just lie here in the moist grass watching the butterflies and bumblebees. It is so peaceful and the air is so cool. Sshh, I hear the overseer's gritty voice. I have to go.

Minty

April 1827

Dear Friend,

It is planting time here on the plantation. We never get a chance to rest. Many of the slaves were whipped for not working hard enough. The sun is making my skin burn. Some older slaves are humming songs to forget the pain. Can you hear them? The sunflowers are competing with each other to see who will be the tallest. The master is coming. I have to focus.

Minty

July, 1827

Dear Friend,

It has been three months since I got a chance to write to you. I was sold to Miss Susan to take care of her whining baby. I have to make sure she does not cry or I will get a whipping with Miss Susan's rawhide. She makes me dust and sweep the floors, too. I can sweep but I don't know how to dust with the rooster's feathers. The baby is crying. I have to go.

Minty

August, 1827

Dear Friend,

This baby is getting too heavy for me. She is also very fussy lately. I got whipped twice today because an ant bit her. She rubs her gums a lot, too. Ole Mae says her teeth be coming out soon. I try to sing to her but she doesn't like my songs. Hush, baby, hush. Please don't cry. Miss Susan is sure to come get me now. Hush, baby, please. I have to go.

Minty

20

Dear Friend,

Today I ran away from Miss Susan. She whipped me with the rawhide so badly that I just couldn't take it anymore. It was my fault this time though. I took one of the tempting sugar lumps from her crystal bowl. I never had anything so good. Now I have to deal with this pain in my body and the hunger I am feeling. I have to find something to eat soon. I think I am going to faint.

Minty

September, 1827

Dear Friend,

Do you hear those grunting noises? Well they belong to the little pigs that I have to fight with for potato peelings every day. I have been living with an old sow and ten piglets for the past six days since leaving Miss Susan's. It has been miserable and depressing. I think I am going to return to Miss Susan. At least, I will have hot milk and a few pieces of stale bread to eat.

Minty

23

July, 1831

Dear Friend,

I am back on the home plantation with Master Brodas. Miss Susan brought me back because she said that I was not worth the eight pennies she bought me for. I am glad to be back with my folks and in the open air.

It is summertime now and the sun is angry and so is Overseer Osborne. He makes me plow the cornfields and load heavy wood into wagons. They say that even though I am only eleven years old, I work as hard as any man.

Minty

dear friend,   december, 1834

i am fifteen years old today. old rit made me a scarf from the scraps of her missus' tablecloth. december can be really cold in these parts. we try to keep the children warm with the burlap and flour bags. they tend to get sick first.

it is dark outside and i can hear whispers. they are speaking about following the north star. it is the brightest and shiniest star in the night sky. i want to follow where it leads. maybe, one day, i will.

Minty

MEET THE
AUTHORS

Front row (left to right): Kadin Johnson, Khaila Wint, Michaela Henry,
Standing left to right: Anilah Helenese, Hannah Cotterell, Da'Jaih Palmer, Kaila Jacobs, Milissa Holness
Left: Principal Gracelyn Farquharson   Right: Project Coordinator & Fifth Grade Teacher Judith Jones

31

Kids Are Authors®

Books written by children for children

The Kids Are Authors® competition was established in 1986 to encourage children to read and to become involved in the creative process of writing.
Since then, thousands of children have written and illustrated books as participants in the Kids Are Authors® competition.
The winning books in the annual competition are published by Scholastic Inc. and are distributed by Scholastic Book Fairs throughout the United States.

This is our final year for the Kids Are Authors® competition.
Thank you to all the children who shared their creativity over the years.

For information regarding permission, write to Scholastic Inc.,
Attention: Permission Department, 557 Broadway, New York, NY 10012.

Copyright © 2016 Scholastic Inc.

Scholastic and associated logos are trademarks and/or registered trademarks of Scholastic Inc.

ISBN 13: 978-1-338-13424-7   12 11 10 9 8 7 6 5 4 3 2 1

Cover design by Bill Henderson

Printed and bound in the USA   First Printing, June 2016

Photo p3 © H. Seymour Squyer/National Portrait Gallery, Smithsonian Institution